Vanquish La Bête Noire

Vanquish La Bête Noire

RAJA HADIYAH

authorHOUSE®

AuthorHouse™
1663 Liberty Drive
Bloomington, IN 47403
www.authorhouse.com
Phone: 1-800-839-8640

First published by AuthorHouse   01/23/2012

ISBN: 978-1-4678-8406-8 (sc)
ISBN: 978-1-4678-8407-5 (ebk)

Printed in the United States of America

Dedicated to Rajanae
Je t'aime

"Merci Seigneur pour les petites joies et Merci aussi à tous ceux qui m'ont soutenue de loin ou de près."

Contents

Exposed

Grabbing birds with wings folded like paper planes

It crushed into tiny paths of wounded remains

And when exhaled a poisonous gas of false smiles

Released the doubt that neither one of us could live without our Love

Tossing heads along the feathered hill

Where sleep breathed secrets through the gills

Of fish like swimming dreams a breathless hope not yet redeemed

I flipped a fear of death between the sheets

Dripping traces of an ocean filled with lies

As the clock ticked, ticked, ticked an endless lullaby of time

I watched you slowly on the left

Melt inside the red pulsing theft

Of muscle, blood and veins

It pounds your name

I gave it all, tissue, platelets and pores

As I dipped my feet into those eyes that adored my existence

You thought you were a little more resistant than proven weak

Nude running down the painful street called love

An open valley shaded by trembling knees

That swayed with the breathing of blowing trees

Ten seconds before you had lost your breath, your pace

I had already erased the face

Of each tiny heartbreaking memory

God Has Healed

Your words tiptoed into my life like little children creeping to find secrets

Splashing ever so silently in my tears

Puddles knee high didn't deter you

Your wading arms pushed forward and ceased my fears

Both of us could feel the vibration

Of my broken heart through my panting cries

And when you looked at me beyond the pain

I could see my future breathe within your eyes

A gentle hand stretched out beyond a humble chest

Your heart as red and as pure as a thumping apple

I can trust you and only you for the first time

And so I lay my head softly upon my nest

Gazing upward to your face

The image of an angel breathing so close to me

I now bathe within grace, breaking locks around my vessels

I shed tears and feel free

Unleashed love without the fear

My blinking lids shake drops of relief

As I watch them rolling across your heart

Your heat absorbing my emotion

And your spirit thirsty for something real

I hold you tightly so that you can feel

Every inch of me falling in love

Agony

I shall never let you near my heart again

With your endless firing, hole after hole

My blood pours fossil shaped rivers

Gushing broken thorns and rusty blades

It shall take more than the height of a mountain to peak over the walls that I have erected

Yet have not completely ejected little parts of you

So I stand there throwing memories and percentages of your journey over my surface

My heart leaning against my dreams

Debilitated and defaced, fiddling with the agony

Unforgiving of my state

I rebuild a machine that will thud faster and harder than before

Love proof with no visible doors

My mouth burned a bitter metal

My heart longs to bathe

But now wrapped in sin, an ugly nailed tight tin

He thirsts to float domestically again

Silent echoes from beyond my gates scream" Unbolt your fear; for I am here it is me your fate"

As I stand there with the key

Longing to unshackle my spirit from this heartbroken lunacy

Certain I should let my rebirth in

With one large suspended teardrop beneath my chin

My bereaved face trills a bleeding dark blue ink

Ceasing the impulse to think of HIM and all that he has been

The author of the darkest tainted dream

That I have ever lived

Piping Rarities

The torment endured through millions of pacing mortal breaths

Can blow out with an inhale one simple backward death

A fire I never thought would die, bent and then singed the eye

I learned yesterday that tears are mucus, water and oil

I thought they were pain

What do I know?

They also contain natural antibiotics

I guess I'm infected

Those diamond ejected catastrophes, hypnotic effects of the cause

The resemblance of me spoiled

They are just mucus, water and oil

Rippling records on the ocean

Piping Rarities

Le Petit Nicholas

Love curled knees bent inside the plasma

Gasped peace and then blinked goodbye

Life played cards on the softness of my abyss

As I sent a deep and mental kiss

My tot felt their first lullaby

I don't have much time to chat

So I'll mumble how things could have been

The gurgle you hear makes it hard to apprehend my words

They say that they can't separate the curds

That holds us apart

So I'll ignore the scary coats and frantic orderlies

Those papers were inked without a choice

Apparently there is no voice in urgency

It was essential to ransom you or me

Those loud red drips are somewhere between life and death

They spin like coins to determine yours or our final breaths

Together entwined bathing between the letters F. A. T.E

You and I are ribs and yes, I saw your knees ever so quickly

You came and shared all of me, all they see, all I'll ever be

Chaos inside the realm, the thirty minute helm

Strength, strength is when you have none left and can still breathe

After having your whole heart taken hastily

Crammed inside the tunnel

Pieces of me wrapped you warmly in my existence

Channeling you safely back to the hiatus

The riotous heart of me

Made it there perfectly and untainted

To the arms of God

Je t'aime pour toujours 01.05.2011

Dismantled

It wondered across the rails

A train that breathes life into fairytales

Of love that imploded inside my chest

Dripping years of insecurity on my thin violet vest

I curled up and listened to my heart ask my knees

If you were me, would you have bent? Would you have run?

I stuck parts of him to the back of my joints

In the back of my arms

Across the lids of my eyes until I couldn't see

And as the dream slowly nibbled at my vital points

I heard a crack as my arms fell, a slow and deadly descent

My knees crashed into tearful repent

Dismantling me

I watched him like a rolling eye

As he scrambled to repair the lie

Standing on my heart he grabbed for my face

A memorable place that absorbed his kiss

His tears a wet streaming evidence that he missed

All of me

Dedicated to my wonderful Father Mr. John D. Gilbert
I love you with all of my Heart

John

Along with the many descendants of great characters
I bloomed through the wisdom of this man
I danced to the tune of a leader, a child of God
With words that flow to the tune of drums
He has healed every sore, every broken heart
He has the eyes of a soldier, a survivor of his faith
With me I carry his tears
They feed the vines that surround my heart
I plant my garden here
With hands that look much like his
His feet are the meadows, the seasons in which I learned to dance
A field of footprints that I choose to walk
His shoulder, a mountain that echoes my cries
A pillow beneath his neck that I have held for years
The ears of a valley filled with emotion
The prettiest that I have ever looked is the reflection in his eyes
His knees have been a painting that I choose to paint
The legs that I now bend to pray
Along with the many leaders of this world
I am the pupil through the teachings of a legend
A man of his time
I dance to the tune of a Shepard, a child of God
I am the daughter of John

Breaking the Chains

The brain swells within the wounds of its cuffs

Bleeding an esteem that was once stolen physically

Pulling the spirit of bronzed skin to its knees

Only the wind remembers the cries that swam between the trees

Of the ones that died before us

We are a race that has been sadly defaced

By those who have never lived beyond the knowledge of their fear

To be dominated by a blood born much greater

And so we humbly take the pin

That pierces the skin in a society that profoundly wish they were like you

Spreading creams that reflect a fallacious sunlight

Envy has boxed their lips into Botox

Graduating into a brighter hue

Of false tans and full smiles

A spirit taken and now an image

As they proudly strut your skin, your man, your child

A phase that should have only lasted a while

And instead of taking back your pride, your stride

Your hips, and the way the brother dips her

To the sound of your jazz

With a little less pizazz then, what it is when he's with you

You abandon your skin too

Dividing into a mixed perception

Of what happiness should be, without the labor and the pain

Of having to fight for what's rightfully yours

You flaunt their hair as they proudly wear your shame

The mass of your kinks, your full lips, your stride

At least as slaves they preserved the pride

But what do you have today?

If you hold neither your mind nor skin

Or the force within to break the chains

Extinguishing the flames, that burns your history

Confiance en Soi

Someone with no esteem is the most dangerous human being

An embellished soul with nothing left to lose

They fuel consistently on others

Everyone that meets them will take the blame

They'll take part in cleaning the stains

From a past where they never learned to love

Not others, but themselves

They walk aimlessly on a ground

Where sounds like advice and notions

Pointing in directions where thirsty souls

Feed off of oceans full of ambition swiftly pass their ears

They hold on relentlessly to the non-evolving position

Of consumer, clinging to every lit soul

That burns like a flame

Smothering the fire within them

So that they can remain, alive

There is no pride inside their shell

And the world they've built within their mind

Is a living hell that chokes the human zest with its

Creamy deadly smoke

And even after years of promises and declarations

They sit and watch us choke, breathless within their need

To feed their crippled self esteem

Someone with no respect is the most dangerous human being

A coated soul with nothing left to lose

A complex lost and confused inside a maze

Holding on to them will lead you to misery

Their destitution is no phase that will pass with the wind of change

But a reconstruction that only the entity can unfold and recondition

Blowing life so that they may exist once again

A perfect ego inside the man

That's healthy enough to love himself

Beyond defrauding a growth, he'll be reborn inside the oath

With new meaning

Gravity

Sometimes the clouds come after the rain

I just can't appreciate you right now; your weight just ate my force

And you need these smiles and validation

When I'm weighed down with remorse, there are these funerals

From little deaths, they just keep dropping off inside my head

Passed out with fatigue, can't you do that yourself?

I mean the thinking part, because the neediness is pushing us apart

And two glasses of wine just doesn't feel like Mozart anymore

You leave mothers, to find mothers, to make mothers

And then you are trapped inside of this world of rational beings

That makes seeing your faults so vivid, so conflicted by the need to be a man

And at the same time lead us, as we try to bury the mess that's already made

I keeping feeling the wade, the wade in the water

And I'm getting sick, the motion, the instability pulls those clouds in

And now they're so thick, that I can't see you anymore

And there you are, cutting through the canvas singing Sinatra

And I just keep falling under the spell of your mantra

Leading us back to square one and I never got to bury those bags

I just keep dragging them to dinners, on vacation, through love making

Even though you've forgotten the pain

The clouds still keep coming after the rain

So I just can't appreciate you right now, your weight just ate my force

And you need these smiles and validation, when there's this other source

Sewing black funerals, from all these little deaths

Constantly absorbed by torn sponge inside my head

I'm passed out with fatigue, can't you do that yourself?

Not just the thinking, but everything else

That puts the weight on me

The Subordinates

We don't wake up there, high up on the mountains looking down on acid rivers

And it probably took some time and a few partners

We don't always get it right the first try

Some of us learn valuable lessons like letting go, while you fly high above riding your bloated ego

And the joys of being grounded even after you lost your pack

And your map got smudged with the tears, is that you get to overcome the fear of losing

Knowing that once their gone, learning how to move on actually liberates you

No longer glued to the cliché, you enjoy painting little black doors in your world

Leading to endless opportunities, directions that the ones like you

Claim to have gotten right the first try

As you swiftly breezed by, because somebody said that black doors lead to nowhere

Ten blessings vanished as they grasp the human fear of image

Teaching you that the darker things are banished

And as you slowly climb the mountain, the wiser ones have vanished

Behind the grey clouds, not a perfect path but the crows belt aloud

And as their echo breaks the fog, it makes ten years of no dialogue worth the pain

So now I stand up on the mountain, watching you lost within the crowd

Of cloned plastic drones, heading upward through the clouds that leak my tears

Your skin absorbs the fear that I once held

And you'll arrive supported by the peak, built miraculously for contrived drill

And you'll be asked what you learned while standing still inside perfection

A perception better placed aside and killed

For the chance to embrace the pain of letting go, clutching faith, healing wounds

To know what it takes, to give in to heartache, cancelling the show

Knowing that you may have missed the first try

Yet the last is the golden conception

Don't laugh at my journey

Rather cry over your confession amongst the subordinates

A Thousand Views

A thousand pairs of tiny fluttering lids

Browsed within my dome

Tearing through secrets, whistling tunes

Swimming inside my habitual thoughts

Voyaging through each tiny room within me

A thousand of the curious kind

Bent the arch of my abstract mind

Lighting flames along the darkest parts of me

As they scrutinized to see who I really am dragging each of my words

With a different harmony inside their heads

Some bringing them to life

Others reminded of the dead parts inside themselves

We all have hidden shelves within the somewhere

Gliding along the tracks of our souls

A thousand tiny scrolls

Down each page the speed of recollection somehow caused an infection

Eating through the prose

Word after word deciphering insanity and rage

The taboo you that's been hidden for years

Yet still suddenly reappears over and over again

As her poems comprehend what others wont

A thousand fans snapping two thin layers of bone and skin

Riding with luggage on their backs

Gazing through the thin walls and fog

Rediscovering themselves inside of the burning snow

A Man's View

I love you and my spirit wants you

Although you drag me through the impossibility of endless screams with dissatisfaction

My actions are not hired; it's how nature wired me

Not the lies, those are my imperfections

But my desire for her perfume is honestly not my intention

Punishing honey bees for noticing lilies between the trees is simply cruel

This is a duel between my nature and your insecurities

Yes you're beautiful and I notice your rarity

But it hasn't blinded me, as I have been given the gift to appreciate a variety of women

While you hastily deem it forbidden to simply look at them

Not become a friend or anything more

I respectfully peer beneath my brow, so that the idea doesn't catch your view

I make efforts not to hurt you with my nature, as I bend with her curves that block the wind

You search to entrap me in the sin of man

I stand in a pool of beauty, marvelously sprinkled by creation

Magnetically drawing every male species

A profound mystery, an indefinable history

That secretes this hidden chemistry that neither love nor comfort can counteract

Causing me to reject, the one thing that was placed inside the man

Not just a ravenous state of attraction, but a transparent dust that transcends

A cheap tasteless lust or the nude imagination

It dives deeply within natures plan for procreation

My apologies are sincere, and so is my fear of losing you

Due to the one factor where I have no control

Although I fight it regardless unlike the heartless

With every passing day I need this love to be stronger than this reality

A man less idealized is just a man that pretends that he can't see

While making you believe that to love truly he must be blind, completely unreceptive to the female

I stand against my manhood

Placing my back and shoulders against the adaptation of pleasing you

I love you but what can I do

When you drag me through the impossibility of endless screams and dissatisfaction

My actions are not hired; it's how nature wired me

Not the lies, those are my imperfections

But my desire for her perfume was honestly not my intention

Punishing gliding birds for noticing the colorful wings that extend a perfect reflection

Would erase the face of nature

I admit, if I exaggerate a bit, I may need a swing or a whack

And as a Gentleman I should never behave like swine

So please don't let my weakness define, or erase your beauty

Vert Blades

I played there inside of it and slid upon it when the clouds wept

And when Mother Nature blew against their tears

Making their grains dry, I'd lay between their tiny arms talking to the sky

Wrapped in pure serenity, they'd tell me secrets and I'd giggle

As their siblings tickled my ears, spinning me into playful rolls of bliss

As the trees jealously hissed, I'd protect them from the large objects they'd throw

Smashing my green blades of family below

The comrades that played with me on Sundays, I wish I could have saved them

When the parents of the soft breeze sped through angrily searching

Tearing apart the trees, lifting roofs looking down inside

As families would fearfully cry, curled up inside their homes

I wish the children of the breeze weren't so bad

Making days like that so sad for all of us

I'm forced to stay inside alone

But tomorrow both my family and I along with others

Will help to clean up the mess they made

And after all the work is done, we'll play once again in the shade

Just as we do on Sundays, just as before Mr. and Mrs. Breeze sped by

We'll stare into the sky, keeping secrets, as endless time rolls a spade

Humming the hymns of Sunday as they grab my feet

I run through the vert blades

That have become my eternal comrades

My Turn

I venture alone inside of my neighborhood

Digging holes and building cities far and high

Windows exploding with secrets

Long metal objects damage doors as they pry

Entering into the dark rooms inside they sped

But the locks are dead

And they climb scissor legged in thievish crime

One black glove leaves a leather smell

Another hand undressed penetrating the well

Two birds one stone

It all can't be done at once

My thoughts rush three in a bunch of millions

Their tiny groups I learned to compartmentalize

Placing them individually, I arrange them size by size behind the dream

Hidden ever so deeply along those endless roads with wooden sheds

Clearing away the cobwebs

That grasp the things I choose not to remember

A masked image of splendor

I stand in line, waiting patiently behind

For my turn

Pedo-Pill

Grabbing a first breath, swimming through the unknown growth of maturity

An oath that promises an age ascending into tomorrow's future

Protected by the ones that know what's best

Yet raping the innocent chest of the child is yet to find a cure

Little knees hide behind greens doors

Tearing eyes that have seen against their will

The desperate need for the Pedo-Pill

Erasing everything both inside and out

Black tears streaming along the throat

Silently trembling each drop into a gut full of secrets

A remote and unhealing world for little boys and girls to start their story

Broken nails softly ripped against the desperate grip of « Don't tell mommy »

The sun falls hiding painfully his burning face from the evil thievish place

Where no one knows the tale of pale sinful regurgitation

I watch the footsteps of a nation gone to wars on substantial budgets

Young men and women fight for things unreal

Yet still no funds toward the Pedo-Pill

Now fourteen years elapsed

After the scratchy beard of innocent theft has killed our dreams

Yellow pills will heal the darkness

while mastering adulthood becomes a carcass flying through the air

A stench that indicates the brains changing gear

Landing us on floor sixteen, Stabler Ward for those who want to kill

Tiny lines of water shots and jackets and still no Pedo-Pill

Suicide becomes option number five

And while we're in there screaming echoes of ghostly cries

Those seekers for soft skin that smells like bubble bath

Their heads thrown back with hungry acid laughs

Prey on thousands more laying on the white stiff sheets

I feel my feet wash against the shore with wrinkled cuts that dry against the chill

Six police cars and a fire truck arrive and still no Pedo-pill to erase my hard drive

The last face that I saw was the editor

Subconsciously erasing the predator, as I sliced through every vein

Feeding sand a last blood filled meal; I died beneath the moon, without the Pedo-Pill

That protects the child that was once me

This Time Around

I feel HIM everywhere, this time around

Blowing ever so lightly I inhale the majestic energy

Arms folded across my chest, hands pressed against my knees

Three times I press my chief on lower ground

My prayer becomes a sound that connects the weight of my faith

This time around

There's and air that joins my thoughts beneath the hood

Embracing vibrations more understood, they debate my state

And spiritually agree upon my fate, I now ordain

A dragging thread above the walk pegged damnation

I lift my knees if only to remain ideal, less culled by temptation

This time around

And with each length of wool I knit my sanctuary

Where broken shells have scattered millions of tiny teeth beneath my feet

Waiting to devour my squandered pace, I clutch my eyes in an attempt to erase all of the sloth

This time around

I stand and try not to fiddle the rushing thoughts that puppet my fingers with anxious frenzy

Breaking the pictures and burning each one, four corners of narrow suns

Hugging with such longing betwixt and between, cleaning all that I've seen

This time around

I burry my heart with shovels and pat the soil firmly placing stones

Watching the beat breaking its cover, with hope to be recovered by HIS will

I stand still inside of nothingness

This time around

I have found inside each vein, a hiding place I've had for years

A scamp dangling alongside the blue ball of ocean that obediently will not fall

With respect for His volition, where I had lost the position

A race sadly frowned upon by the galaxies

This time around

So I brush my knees and let my spirit circulate within my broken walls

Six feet and a few feet tall of lost embrace

Yet when I look deeply through my face

I peak behind a past where my ignorance was defined

As a cordless violin dancing to ancient sounds

I cradle me inside of myself, a human reality

That my existence unfolds with or without my resistance

This time around, I am a Woman

Young Man a Woman's Plea

Here I am broken and unsure

There are two windows left, life closed the other doors

And my tears dried up with all the painful screams

And the fear burned out with all the dreadful dreams

And now he tells them stories that aren't true

Of things I know he's sure I didn't do

But he's tired of me seeming like a priest, so he feeds on me like a final feast

So alas for once he'd appear to be good

And so they'd listen and he'd feel more understood

But what they don't see is the truth beneath the lie

And how he manipulates with false words while he cries

Yet deep inside he knows that they can't see, that all this mess took more than only me

And the hate he's had stored sleeping there for years

And all the nights he held back all his tears

A childhood of memories that were grey

Haunting him with every passing day

Finally he has found someone to blame, for all the years he's carried all the pain

Eyes dripping with uncertainty

With his fear he holds on tight to me

And tells them all that he's standing on his own

Pretending that independence is all he's ever known

As I carry him on my tiny back even though I've lost the force

And the roads are long and keep on changing course

And like him my visions blurred and I can't see

But I keep walking knowing all he has is me

So he yells and tells me I'm no good

And that his life is hell and he'd walk alone if he could

I feel the tears keep rolling down my face

And I quickly start picking up the pace

He's getting heavy and I feel like I can't breathe

I've fallen many times and torn apart my knees

Yet no one is here to hear my painful cry

I'm just the Femme that's carrying the guy

Sadly this is all that they will ever see

They'll never notice that someone beneath, The Me

Carrying the boy that becomes a man

The boy that's still afraid to stand

They'll keep telling him to walk ahead alone

"Don't look back boy" she's just a stepping stone

And even though she seemed so sweet to you

And made your red skies turn perfect blue

You're growing now, so move on boy it's time

Cut the root and hang on to the vine

She'll find her way just as she always does

Healing herself forgetting all that was

Oh dear boy, none of this is true

The bruises inside my heart are stained and blue

So even though you've grown and built your pride

The woman you rode to get there "Yes me"

Gets washed out with the tide

And the only trace you'll carry in your hand

Are the footsteps I left behind in the sand

Along with the blood that was dripping from my feet

As I carried you until the journey was complete

And just as your feet had hit the ground

And the ocean had barely made a sound

And the crowd starting clapping just for you

And I was no longer in their view

You smiled quite proudly as you took a bow

An accomplishment all thought was only yours

As I drowned helplessly, weak and tired beneath the shores

And my memory is the imprint of my back

Pasted wrinkled dirt, with my sweat between the cracks

Of your shirt, drying rapidly against the breeze

And your aching fate, a pain acquired by bending your knees holding on

As I hobbled out of love into your dreams

Burned by sun rays and held up by their beams

I love you, never proved to be what it seemed

As the water filled my breathless neck

My lungs exploded like a wooden deck

With my shoulders hitting the ocean floor

As the waves opened up the oceans doors

Humming sounds my soul had never heard

Raising it up above you like a bird

And just when you believed that I had disappeared

God formed a ME without the pain and the fear

And the traces of footprints that you passed along the sand

Where no longer the footsteps I made when I could stand

But larger ones for everyone to see

I am Your Mother, I am your Wife, I am your Sister, I am your Daughter

And this time Young Man, it was God that carried ME

Dedicated to my beautiful Mother Willamae
"The gates of heaven lies beneath the mother's feet"

Elrina

I dream inside your skin, literally lean inside of it and travel

To far off places where no one has been

Your voice aligned everything, inside of me

Within every form of you I mellow

Seamed eternally to Elrina

In your hands I find the trace

That sketches the defining face of my existence

And without these tracks there are no prints

No scattered hints that I once breathed here inside a womb so dear

Before a breath began my death

I lived inside Elrina

I grabbed her scent preserving it, dashed it on the surface of the sea

And marveled gaping its reflection

As I blushed a mirror of perfection

Honored to have seen

The soul of Elrina

I watched it freeze as even the earth

Scrambled to defeat the breeze

Wanting so much to scatter you everywhere, if only to enhance the beauty throughout the plains

Watching rare flowers suddenly appear

Again, again and again, with the scent of Elrina

I cuddled in the trees that wore your arms

And fell upon the rain

I mixed your tears with them if only to sustain your breath

Inside a world that wants to one day claim your death

So gracefully leaving me to explain proficiently

That I had one day seen her, this beautiful butterfly called Elrina

And so I cry eking words a purple hue

Deriving letters turning them around and upside down

Spelling things that could only describe "You"

Like no one else has ever been depicted

I stand convicted in the impossibility of this misdemeanor

There will never be words to describe Elrina

She is like no other, and I am honored to have her as my mother

The Salient Elrina

The Man

I dragged a chair to his fore, crossed my legs and lit a bulb

Blew away some tissue searching deep within his core

Now what I found astounds me and I think it's a quantum leap

As I swam around inside his head, whilst he pilgrimaged through his sleep

Unlike some I used protection as I ventured through the brain

Found some things I shouldn't mention

Including missing plugs labeled "Refrain"

This discovery explained mountains, I thought, as I laughed but swam along

Past all of the gray and murky matter of bristly testosterone

Falling through an empty space, warm and dark with lies

I landed on what must be the tongue, filled with unexplained goodbyes

Almost losing all my gear I advanced at cautious pace

Trying not to be befuddled by such an admirable face

Crossing arms athwart my chest I took the grisly slide

To a place that he claims only I abide

A muscle filled with reddish blood, pounding amity and fear

This must have been the only space authentic and sincere

I wish I could have stayed inside and taken all my needs

But in me there's another side filled with untold curiosity

So pressing against his chest, I took another bound

This time the journey seemed drawn out, but I didn't make a sound

Bracing myself for the uncharted

Where could the next stop be?

A bounce and then a feathered swoop, landed me assuredly

A mysterious tissue washed out pink and white

Cushioned my plump behind from a baggy midair flight

Now here's a zone that baffles me

I'm now confused as to where I stand

And the only way to locate the map, is within the mind of the man

So I looked around for something familiar, some evidence, a gland or bone

And like the ocean I rose and fell with echoes of cries and groans

There it was, to my surprise bigger than a grain

I had already passed the right side first and voilà! The left side of the brain!

This is quite odd I must admit

And far too low in the body to be legit, this must effect his health

And for hours I sat there trying to make the analysis by myself

The left side of the brain in here? Inside the tunnel without a bone

Everything to this point had been so utterly clear

The brain naturally occupies the gates locked between the ears

Now here it is inside the chute

The idea made me quail with fear

And on the walls read names of females written cheaply everywhere

I shuttered with flutters as my heart sunk ever so painfully and deeply inside this ghostly cave

I now fathom where I stand

Brushing my feet angrily inside the second mind of the man

Disgusted and tired I turned around and searched to climb from whence I came

To the warm and refined heart that for years withheld my name

But my legs and my mind where terribly weak

And I felt completely torn apart

The reality of my discovery notably heavy left me with a broken heart

So with one little sneeze and a whisk of a breeze

I was finally emancipated

On a stiffened muscle I was pushed out the gate, as I was swiftly ejaculated

Irretrievable

I watch them age
Each wrinkle and arc entraps me
With the perturbing hug of detachment
Elicited by years of not witnessing the process
The distance bleeds my heart
An absent stroke of art within their realm
On my knees now overwhelmed
I stroke the painful ache with a brush that tries to change its fate
And restore the years whilst I wasn't there
Breathing inside a space of romantic atmosphere
Chasing a dream
Wrist bent passionately with each stoke of Chroma
Simply to redeem the thick aroma of buoyant age
With what wage could I now pay to get it back?
To touch their faces, burrowed inside that secure place
A sanctuary with ears that store my bones
The telephones no longer fuel the crave to hold them near me
And remember clearly their heartbeats
Instead I sit and watch them age
Each wrinkle and arc entraps me
With the perturbing hug of detachment
Elicited by years of not witnessing the process
The distance bleeds my heart, an absent stroke of art
Within their realm
I'm so overwhelmed as I stroke the painful ache
Painting a golden gate upon the canvas in my mind
Running sticks along their bars
A tune that for now channels a chime
Ringing routinely until I see them again
Witnessing the irretrievable

❧ RAJA HADIYAH ❧

Woman of Islam

Salaams, but not dunks in a basket

Heralding peace in the form of a whisper

Humbly secured in the tidings that affirms her habituate faith

She covers her face retaining her place within the divine abode

Not a hiding place but armor, protecting her from the defiled spirit of the defiled

The All Knowing, sanctions those who He wills with understanding

The misunderstood place of the submissive

Who daily make amends within their truth

Her beauty hidden from the tooth of their large mane

She sustains her innocents

And her ears bypass the eavesdrop of the degrading whistle

Not a cloth that hides a missile, but a silk that rests softly against her skin

Revealing to others a reflection of her soul

A voice heard louder than a half dressed woman in the cold

As men speak with eyes that reflect an open breast

Women cry endlessly for respect

An act less practiced by themselves

Handing a spoon rendering it easier to be devoured by her prey

Within a carnal modern society today, they continue to mock those who are hidden

A woman that peacefully claims her esteem

By covering all that is seen

Fights a law deeming it forbidden to respect her flesh

An act punishable if chosen to refrain from following a faith

That allows her to obtain harmony

So what exactly would you like to see?

As you banish her from public for not revealing her legs

And arrest the prostitute for lying on bags, in the back seats of cars

After hanging around the bars that the state has funded

You now want to create a law that makes modesty redundant

So what must a female do?

If she can neither remain covered or undressed

Salaams, but not dunks in a basket

Heralding peace in the form of a whisper

Humbly secured in the tidings that affirms her habituate faith

Please let her cover her face

Retaining her place within the divine abode

Not a hiding place but an armor protecting her from the defiled spirit of the defiled

With the heart of God simply try to understand

That a Woman is more than being desired physically by a man

She remains covered to retain her respect

In a society that views the female as something far less

Than Royalty

Blank Walls

There are days when I duel to squeeze it out

Riot swing with me for just another span in endless time

The distant ticks, the clocks, the effrayant chime

DONG!

I search for moments less determined

And when found I'll wait inside their chin

The wind takes age and stretches it

Escaping freely a criminal ageless skin

Yet no one will arrest him

I'm sure the culprit is "le vent"

For all of life's mishaps

Tick tick tick

A moment cannot remain idle

Except for junctures like this

If I could only escape the bliss, for a second

I'd push out more I reckon

Conventional needs to read

If only to plant my seed

Inside the semicircular area above your necks

There will always be days like this

Fighting to squeeze it out

When the tiny footsteps on my clock

Keep tiptoeing about inside my head

Numbers and distance all aligned

Chaos swing with me for just another span

Within the endless time of a writers blank walls

Rebirth

His love envelopes me

Sealing me inside the veins of courage

Bathing my spirits in the sparkling realm of the unconditional

And with all that's additional, it feels like heaven here

Cuddled beneath the surety of his kiss

Where windows dance an adjacent bliss

Mirrored I feel so warm and smile over the love that was born

Inside this dream

I can breathe his skin each sheet of lengthened masculinity

A kindred spirit age old senility can never make me forget

My breaths in his arms

Back slouched and head a swinging humility, he unarms me

Stripped down lace by lace

His voice echoes within the little space

That I occupy in our crowded realm

Scaling the the outskirts of earth

He is my final rebirth

Within the heart

Prediction

A large breath and then I'll let go of everything that resembles

Swirls of color when black and white were two devoted worlds

Like bowls with two weak sides they'd collide

Creating such a beautiful explosion

A splash of evanescence between the emptiness

We held the essence of something real

Arms wide and then collapsed to both sides deflated

Can't tell which side was hated the most

Those cries were simply a host

To its final end

Swindlers Contortion

Swindler rides on windy mountain roads that climb the highest peak

His noisy tongue is where you'll find his abode

Dripping like thunder at your feet

Mimicking stories or better yet confusion

It's contorted, best left aborted

Inside the illusion of Swindler's Contortion

Swindler the pink flexible spoon between your teeth

Has rotted your face, flapping flags on winds of grace

An odor that's destroying the healthy home

How could the sustainer have forgotten?

That Swindler sadly won't work alone inside the story

He'll build heaps of worry and he must be courted

By others like himself

Swindler takes what's ours and it all becomes contorted like lui même

The afflicted elf

A beautiful story with well lived trials

Bumpy dens with flowers inside of them

They hide from friends that rape the face

But Swindler somehow finds their fate and leaves it all contorted

Blue Valley

There's a blue valley that appears willfully

Not a bright light, like the heavenly extinction

But a valley long and half grey

Should I choose that one today?

I laugh loud with cheerful blasts of electric pants

Cramped filled joys of corner slanted smiles

You kill me with your humor; I impress you with my poise

I chose the blue valley today

I shuffle my feet to the sound of yellow birds

And to a jargon that you've never heard

Accept when you hang there drunk thinking you have just enough spunk

To decipher the difference between hooting owls and quacks

As you slide upon your back inside your demon

Three decades of evolved semen, you sit and waste

Thinking in patterns of grey

You should have just taken the blue valley

Like me today

Home

Finalement! A word less bled in lighter shade of gray

In the right back corner of my head

Blue butterflies and purples trees

I prayed there once without knees

The grass was wet; afraid to slip I tugged the net

That he promised me ever so securely in the rainy world

Sunny days were filled with cucumbers and pommes de terre

I grew them myself

Boiled them on days when nudity beset my shelf

Hot water always makes amends between the gardener and her friends

Ils sont ma famille

I lay them on my chest reading melodies

Of old French tomorrows, or was that yesterdays?

I found my quarters when I arrived

Didn't know which way was town

As I stood there in my gown

Thinking, finalement!

I am home

Adieu

I absorbed at least ten gallons of it

Thunderous impulses and two bags of genius wit

Choked a few times, but I guess I didn't chew

My teeth were soft from agony of which were not a few

Deep breaths once saved my life, to be exact more times than none

Flaming hairs inside my chest hotter than the sun

A ball that rose and gulped on its decent

Muscle arched inside my back where all the bucking went

Fingers bathed in humidity but dried between the wind

Waving frantically at him

Au revoir mon amour

Knuckles pale

I'm just not sure

Where the rapture went

Must have lost it on the balls decent

Inside my throat

That is torn with grief

Saying Adieu

Static

He's chasing it

No, not the dragon

Those little funny currents

Hopping across the room sliding on his furry chest

Invisible arrows direct his playful way

East, west

Static trapped outside the TV screen

Nature almost seems mean

Sizzling sounds augmenting the illusion

What clever confusion outside of his head

My pour little furry friend feels dizzy now

Purring marbles with triangles intimately inside of them

One facing upward, the other downward

A perfect leap sends him gliding across the room

But just a bit too soon

Sliding down the wall

The static is ten feet tall

My furry friend

He's still chasing it

No, not the dragon

Those little funny currents

Static trapped outside the TV screen

Psychosis

Quick blinks clearing out cobwebs

Left to right, side to side

Did I just separate the two directions?

Do they have a remedy that fights infections inside of me?

The psyche

Quick pace, breaking the invisible chains

They left me pained in the bed inside my head

Forgot to straighten out the sheets

Quick beats, heart racing

Steady pacing as I tip from side to side

Eyes wide but can't see a thing

Detached floating there with metal wings

Quick flaps but I can't fly

I can't glide because my sheets are pink

And with four more quick blinks they are green

Quick flashing scenes

Quick flash, quick flash

And then I cry

Six months somehow went by since the last tear

Quick blinks squeezing out the fear

That protects me inside my head

My soul floats dead

Breathlessly inside psychosis

Secrets

The sensation of the secret
Chronic joy that bends the rain
Shutting eyes of sickened viewers
Looking down from grassy plains
There's a whistle in the sunset
Blushing clouds with Tuesday's rhyme
Thick extremities rend them nearer
Grabbing tight the hands of time
And the drops that roll like silk
Off the mane of muscled men
Whisper chimes of sweet sensation
Bringing secrets to no end
Shhhhhh

The Good Book

It captured me, the words the prose

I sat there cemented in the author's sphere

Submissively I let him take me everywhere

Inside the dream

Within the trees

Sitting on the branches high above where he fell in love

With his dame

I met my minds expansion

As I captured every scene

I smelt her hair and her voice

That led me to his artery

Escaping all the parts of me that sat there reading in public

Noisy cars and scraping feet

The sound of dry brittle sheets

Of interruption

A brow secreting its intensity

And the complexity of love

Written between the hardbacks of sublime novelty

And as I slid down from the tree

Capturing his last whispers to her

Inhaling the memory

The bus arrived

No Doubt I Loved

I loved you, I loved all of you

Each one conflictingly

The ones inside of you and externally

I loved them

Even the ones that disarmed me

Taking my cells and my platelets

Leaving my throbbing palate

Completely carved for the universe to absorb within its natural orb

It's been cosmic swimming through the realms

Although I stepped out dry

What was wet stayed left inside the passion

The memories arched beneath the stars

When I lengthened my back in your embrace

A perfect image of me

Curiosity

Curiosity compels them

Like a growling gut

Strut after strut

Piercing through the windows of my life

Tipping wine glasses to strife and burning the photos of joy

Pretending to be so coy

As they twist the images of destiny

Their unchanging fallacy

Kissing cheek to cheek

Transferring the odor of envy

That builds in cups and basins

Oceans that rot at their depths

As they hold their poisonous breaths

Curiously staring in on moi

C'est moi qui porte la croix

And the torment

Of their gossiping tongues

Insight

Write them pleasant they kindly asked

Poetry without flowers? How can I grasp

The concepts of blood and agony

If I myself have not preserved through such misery

Dancing on my own boring thoughts

A purchase so plainly bought

For the price of happiness

Will I be so sadly missed?

When eternity trails me back into space

I cipher the pace of my aging

Through ten steps of wisdom that I somehow acquired

Leaving seven corners of my soul on fire

And the other heaps of snow

A brilliant reflection of my light

They'll say "She had awkward Insight"

Didn't she?

Into the heart and the minds of the human

The Focus

The focus, the focus that crippled our genius ingenuity

They stand there fixated on a lie

Entangling bit by bit each coil from left to right

The mind has nearly lost the fight

As focus stares wide eyed in fright

Reality leaves the interpretation

A battle, sub grabs conscious pinning him down

The weight, the gear

The fight started when sub made conscious believe

He was actually going somewhere for good

Love, kids, plans

Sub selfishly piles his garbage on all of them

The deceit when as I really believed

That sub was my best friend

Taking all of me for me

Corralled up inside myself

He built these shelves

And so neatly systematized my everything

Hypostasizing the bulbous sting I called my brain

Not leaving a trace, a crumb or a stain inside my head

On the cushioned sides of it

He fucked me, giving back all my shit

Once again

Sub was a fallacious friend

Silver Rain

Lightening flashing across the inner lining of my solitude

A prelude to other verses that told tales of hidden pasts

Slightly fading like sun rays I erase them all at last

Underneath the breath of his kiss

Wide hands that perch my mind on a pedestal of wild emotions

Love and exploding veins like a hungry ocean

Secret cities that open doors to things once said

In his soul I make my bed

And cry tears in reverse

Climbing out of the steady rolling hearse

I am no longer dead

Neither pale beneath the darkened skies

I no longer bat my lids with burning eyes

I no longer slide my fingers across the bruise

Of simultaneous heart wrenching news

I make love to bells of silver rain

Under moonlit horoscopes he says my name

And when I hear his soul crying out for me

And smiling down with such sincere vanity

I know that his love is true

Sick Hound

Fear, the fearless prisoner

Shackling the love sick hound

Swollen hearts that bleed dripping over blue wounds

Screaming and leaping the rage of baboons

Paper cut hair ripping through his hands

Cutting nerves that still don't make him understand

That she breathes, she is, she exists

Although fallen to her knees

Tears that swim between the blood and the trees

Fear, the fearless prisoner

That breaks each of her legs

That ties her peg like arms

Far beneath her bloodied gaze

She loves him

Even though she cannot leave

And with his hands held tight around her throat

She cannot breathe

Yet she inhales Fear, the fearless prisoner

Shackling the love sick hound

Pointing fingers in two directions

One to death

The other heaven bound

Puddles

Love a word that sounds, sounds like a bell chiming in the wind

Letters curling on the tongue

Twisting passionately beneath the summer sun

Of tomorrows heartache

Knees bent above the puddles of tears

The mountain of mistakes

The rivers splashing ever so elegantly with rippled fears

He cut me as deep as a knife

Rutted edges tearing through my throbbing muscle

Leaking bloodless veins filled with air

Into the dark grey atmosphere

It rained sorrow

As my spirit evaporated

Salty drops with lost tomorrows

He hates me

As love dissipates in me

A sizzle and then all dry

As the last drip of bloodless veins deny

That love once flowed here

Simply to Feel the Peace

Lids burning from inside

Shaking skin that takes my breath

My spirit rides the waves of what feels like backward death

And so my tears run inward and my thud pounds deep inside

Fists of anger from the past that diminished all my pride

I stand there but my mind won't walk and my knees forget to bend

Childlike I swim in regression clueless without possessions

While impulse sends a sign to run throughout a land where there is no Sunday

The darkness a thin line across my pupil where God's brush still paints a face

The unfamiliar print of another race of inner ME's one after the other

Neither of them a brother beneath this sky where only a graveyard of spirits abide

Filled with souls that remains eternally lost

I would pay any cost, simply to feel the peace

One Eyed Youth

She will never comprehend the goblins

The spooky world that dwells

She dances with ballet spins

Like she is under clueless spells

There's this danger that rides on a grey and foggy wind

That has captured her unformed wings

And she's blown about the forest forgetting what being human means

Protect yourself I tell her

But her ears hear songs of youth

On tiny toes she slips along

With a faith that's shaken loose

So I plead with God to follow only steps behind

Or in front, wherever he sees the need

If only to remind her of all I've taught her

And the things there are to come

And that judgment has no space for two

She will stand as only one

Before him one day

When her days have passed like a season

God I pray that she doesn't wait for you to understand

That her life truly does have meaning

Waiting for you to Love Me

My face stretched gum like with pain

Ten angles to the left with one side trapped in the rain

Quotes and flying notes reminding me

Of all there is and that may not be

The insane writer jogs aimlessly grabbing at her heart

Her stomach fills with blood filled clefs of hateful words

There goes the bluebird snatching a leaf

A sonnet, a piece of her belief or disbelief

He'll carry it gracefully where only God can see

A place where the me inside the me can be free from the struggle

The endless puzzle that always holds a missing piece

My words written over and over again will one day form a sheet

If only to complete the dripping painting

The one on the wall of my chest

I have been wrong, I have sinned and now I long to complete the test on this pathless highway

Signs bent and turned to persuade my direction

Have only led me to imperfection

My bad selection has now made me walk backward with hope

On a slippery land I cope and like trees against the wind I will not bend

I will continue to stand firm again

Waiting for you to love me

Swallowing Memories

His sadness rests on his pillow

Like clouds he sits on them and remains afloat

The words fly from his tongue like sleepless dreamers counting goat after goat while awake

The saddest life ever told

As he spins his large bowl of regrets

He digests it daily as if to never forget all that he lived and he did

Fault after Fault, dream after dream

I long to push him high up on a sunbeam

Placing him under the fluffy feather of a dove

And have him carried to all of the places that he's wished he had seen

To places that even I myself have never been

Erasing every female face that has defaced his cliché

His tears splash packed inside of his fear to live

Leaking questions drop from the sides as he walks

Why did I allow these things?

Every thought takes wings as he swings his frail legs and turns

To the same window that he'd gaze from as a child

When his tears and pain were considered mild

Compared to what he now sees as his end

His only friend has now become his tongue

Shaking hands with his thoughts and sharing them with everyone

A broken heart that continues to swallow its memories

Dripping Wine

The ripping and the tearing I just can't repeat

The healing and the agony of the loss

Each beat inside of me runs from the thought

Waiting for nature to give me a sign

That celebrates the dripping wine

Red but not pleasurable, yet although measurable enough to exhale with relief

At least once escaping the heat of trials

The ones that defile the spirit

Leaving me strong enough to drag my mind along

My heart breathes deeply and tires

I am gold I'm told and must pass through the fire

I long to bathe inside the lake of eternal grace that soothes the wound

Lord command my tube to move

I refuse to repeat the shame

Let me remain inside of grace

I hide my face and ask this one thing from you

If it is a blessing, let it be healthy and new

And I promise to give him back to you

Searching for faith

Dashing from your own reflection

Into what seems so serene

My heart no longer trusts that my emotions have been of good judgment

Hidden beneath fear I break the surface

I kneel there ashamed and worthless

Show me where this faith abides

Scraping and crawling inside myself

My mouth held open without a sound

Screaming internally to the chirps of black crows

Doomed and shot by thin rusty arrows

My pulse begins to fade inside the endless maze

Searching for faith

Gashed Puppet

My fate blew on a grey dusty wind

Surfing a small crumpled sheet of doctrine

Passersby could barely catch a glimpse of my promise, my fate

Stains of lipstick and tears, fingerprinted lust filled fears

Dripped a blue like stain on the cliché

A cord with too much leeway hung me high above where souls must one day fly

To reach their Paradise

An exhibition that bled the ambitious world

I watched the little girl climb from inside of me

Hanging on and then letting go

Catching the breeze and then swiftly shooting away like a destined arrow

Leaving my core to dissipate

I fed the atmosphere with verses, chapters and sonnets

That never reached high enough to loosen my noose

Humming breath into me again

Eyes wide open I watched it all slip away

Even my tears ran along the side of my tongue

Hatefully starving me from the life they once proclaimed

What's my name?

I am fear, I am lust, I am shame, I am hate

My anger built a mountain beneath my feet

It reaches me; it saves me and stands on my faith my, knowledge, my heart

Squeezed lifeless inside a tiny box of pain

Thumping the bows, wetting the tape

My birthday was no surprise they said, it was fate

So sing the song that bellowed and embraced my spirit on the day that I first breathed

When your first words and my name gave meaning to me

Lost, lost inside the realms

Hum their notes so that I may see one day

The path that was chosen

Not the one that you had taken after you had lost your way

Hung above the flames far beneath Paradise, just as I am

A Gashed Puppet

A Tomorrow That Will Never Be

Headaches that absorb pity and create thunderous pounding thoughts

Beating the threads of my locks

Entangling themselves into knotted things that I can't get out of me

From around me or inside of myself

An endless shelf of getting over you

That crazy sin that makes me want to eject everything

Those memories of us scrape the inner part of my heart

And clip the blue veins and the red ones retiring the fire

The flame nearly burned me alive before my tears extinguished the flickering death

The sound of steamy sizzling goodbyes

Still hasn't completely diminished yet

I'm just letting off steam creating sweat evoked streams

Almost deep enough to drown myself

Just one more drip of that insane pain and I'll back stroke

Like air into my vein and implode my own existence

Punishment for my weak resistance against your charming words

Those reasons come like seasons and find me through fiery suns and snowy mountains

I crawl without knees like a herd of bellyless cows

To the top of my mind and huddle into that space

The only place that doesn't smell like you

It's where I have been, where I am, my wild zoo of beast filled sorrow

Gnawing on images of a tomorrow that will never be

Hollow

It's so hollow here

The eternal heeding to his words left me bleeding drizzles that echoed inside my thud

A rapping, constant rapping

Harrowed and impact of reality that swam me to this fatality beneath his shoe

Footsteps in every direction a pain that's new to every corner of my brain

Tiny scratches of hateful words driving me insane

It's so hollow here

Loneliness without his warm painful hatchets

That slide off of me like a thorn filled jacket

Surrendering my fears of death

Disturbed I walked alone inside this multicolored dome bathing my wounds

Wrapping them with the sound of chastity

My fingers had the audacity to stroke in vain

And so a little lower I ventured to abstain from the emptiness I felt

Yet even respectfully beneath my waist below

It is still so intensely mellow just as I feared

It is still so hollow there

Inside the snare that snatches all of them

The unchaste and callus men

That when remembering me become poets that breathe through monster gills

"That is some kind of poison you've got there"

And as I recall, even with them through all of the fights and tears

It remained so hollow there

Inside my heart

Jezebel

I strolled away a back curved to the shape of a D

Only flashes away from you obliterating me

I glimpsed at the blade slowly caressing my back

With a passionate attack that curved your arm landing accurately on your hip

And instead of bleeding me, you danced unfastening the eternal grip of the Jezebel

A violence that had you strutting awkwardly

Staring, dreaming, wondering eyes from your window

Suffering inside your world

Nothing but girls, girls, girls that ransacked your normalcy

A boy that fell victim to the night

And now you sit behind your curtain living vicariously through your sight

Imagining yourself doing things you could never do as you sit there outside their view

Unmasked with insanity

A flower with blade like petals, you hate their vanity

So let them bleed all of the Jezebels, let them heed to your words

You cry for little boys inside your world

And just as men denounced, the women must also pronounce their shame

Of offense that replaces games and toys with insanity

A monster licking wounds with mouths that breathe "Kill them and then kill me"

You fall asleep inside the pain

Humbled by dreams that help you remain "Mommy's little boy"

Someone should have fixed it before you got so twisted between the sheets

Pleasing yourself on images of my face

Sliding further from, whose grace?

Your faith and agitating reminder of your sin

That you have no conscience now

And that your love for me had shattered every vow

Never ever to love the Jezebel

Lullaby

Sleep has come again and the day must finally be eaten by its end

But not the spirit, the spirit breathes slowly and remembers everything that creates the light

Not a pain comes to mind, only singing birds in flight

You're floating on clouds high above this life

And with slow gentle breaths you feel your heart enjoy serenity

Tranquility of the mind that holds on to sonnets and childish rhymes

You feel your stomach jiggle with joke filled giggles from all the funny things you've ever heard

Reflecting, you replace your fear with each word that brings you joy

Like hope, freedom, flowers, health, sunsets

I am youth and have endless opportunities tomorrow

I am standing on a tower high above the ocean with my arms stretched wide

I am the wind around me; I am the tide beneath me

I am breathing a new and endless chance to become all that I have ever desired

My feet are light and my soul is like fire burning through the sunset of my future

A light that warms me like a summer day on the beach

In my mind I feel nature teach me how to live, how to appreciate

I need no one but myself to validate me

I am free, I am happy

I am like bubbles blown around and flowers neatly patterned on the ground

I am trees high above my head, I am not dead

I am reborn over and over again

I hear music of a song that fills my heart with joy

There is no one else but me as I dance

I am a girl, I am a boy, I am a woman, I am a man

I have become more beautiful with age and maturity

And there exists no old in the infinity of the soul

Old is a word boldly used for the ones who cannot remember, or feel the warmth of another

gender

Who can no longer dream of the things that can be felt tomorrow

That's not me, I am smiles, I am laughter, I am never sorrow

Sleep, sleep has finally come and I am smiling because nothing can steal my bliss

I feel peace within the memory of my mother's kiss

For a moment I am ten again and I'm anticipating a new day

New experiences and the possibility of meeting new people

The old me dissipates with every second

I become new with this sleep

I laugh; I count sheep that are labeled with all the dreams I am yet to fulfill

All of the trials I endure are simply just a tiny spill of ruin

My future is soft like a wind blowing silk around my nudity

I am forever free to sleep and be happy

I am wonderful, I am excellence I am perfection that cannot be mirrored

I can sleep and go as deep as my peaceful spirit needs

As I listen to Raja read this poem over and over again